T0286733

What Would You Do?
(Making Good Choices)
Parent's Introduction

We Both Read books have been developed by reading specialists to invite parents and children to interact as they read together.

This book is designed to be read to a child by a parent or adult. Ten scenarios are presented which involve a social and emotional challenge for a character. After a scenario is introduced in the book, parents ask children to make choices about what to do in the situation. Three choices are offered, followed by the questions: "Which one would you choose?" and "Why would you choose that?"

The answer the child provides is not as important as discussing the situation that is presented and understanding the child's choice. We suggest not labeling any choice as "bad" or "wrong." Understanding the reason for the choice can be more helpful.

The child is then shown the choice that the character in the book has made in each situation and ends with two questions: "Do you think the character made a good choice? Why do you think that?" These questions are simply a way to invite discussion about how we can make choices in what we do and how

different actions can affect ourselves and our relationships with others. It can be helpful to point out the positive results of making a good choice, even when it was not an easy choice to make.

Depending on your child, it may be helpful to read only a part of the book at a time. We suggest trying to keep the discussions as positive and fun as possible. Make positive comments about your child's answers to the questions, commenting on the merits of alternative choices. It can often be helpful to ask them to clarify why they think a particular choice is appropriate.

Keep these tips in mind, but don't worry about doing everything right. Simply sharing this book with your child will help them to develop social and emotional skills that will be important in school as well as provide an enjoyable experience for both of you.

What Would You Do?
(Making Good Choices)
A We Both Read® Book: Level K-1

———————————————————————

Text copyright © 2022 by Sindy McKay
Illustrations copyright © 2022 by Meredith Johnson
All rights reserved.

Consultant on Social and Emotional Development:
Iris Sroka, Ph.D.

We Both Read® is a trademark of Treasure Bay, Inc.

Published by
Treasure Bay, Inc.
PO Box 519
Roseville, CA 95661 USA

Printed in China

Library of Congress Control Number: 2021943700

ISBN: 978-1-60115-368-5

Visit us online at:
WeBothRead.com

PR-12-22

What Would You Do?
(Making Good Choices)

By Sindy McKay

Illustrated by Meredith Johnson

TREASURE BAY

Spilled Paint

Rachel and Alex are painting pictures together at the arts and crafts table. Rachel leaves to get a new color of paint and. . . . Oops! Alex accidentally knocks over a paint cup! It spills all over Rachel's painting!

What do you think Alex should do?

Should Alex . . .

. . . tell Rachel he is very sorry and ask her what he can do to make her feel better?

. . . or tell Rachel that a giant fly flew by super-fast and knocked the cup over?

Or RUN?!

Which one would you choose?
Why would you choose that?

Alex decided to tell Rachel the truth. He told her he was very sorry and cleaned up the mess with a sponge.

Rachel was glad that Alex said he was sorry, and she forgave him. Later that day, Alex made some silly hats for them to wear and the two friends laughed together.

If Alex had said there was a giant fly, Rachel might have become really scared!

If Alex had run away, Rachel might have thought someone else had spilled the paint and that would not be fair.

**Do you think Alex made a good choice?
Why do you think that?**

New Girl

There is a new girl in class today. Isabella spots her sitting all by herself at recess. Isabella feels shy about talking to her. But the new girl looks so lonely.

What do you think Isabella should do?

Should Isabella . . .

. . . ignore the new girl and go play on the swings?

. . . or introduce herself to the new girl and invite her play ball?

. . . or dress up like a monster and roar loudly so the new girl won't *want* Isabella to talk to her?!

Which one would you choose?
Why would you choose that?

Isabella knows how hard it is to be new and not know anyone. She gathered her courage and introduced herself.

Then the two girls played ball together.

If she had ignored the new girl, Isabella might have felt sad about how lonely the new girl was.

If Isabella had dressed up as a monster, the new girl might have been scared as well as being lonely.

Do you think Isabella made a good choice?
Why do you think that?

Birthday Bicycle

Tommy's big brother, Phil, got a cool, new bicycle for his birthday today. Tommy asks if he can ride it, and Phil says no. Phil explains that he just got the bike today and tells Tommy he can ride it tomorrow.

What do you think Tommy should do?

Should Tommy . . .

. . . tell his mother that Phil is being mean to him?!

. . . or drape toilet paper all over Phil's new bike?

. . . or respect his brother's wishes and patiently wait until tomorrow?

Which one would you choose?
Why would you choose that?

Tommy thought about how he felt when he got a brand-new toy. Then, as hard as it was, he decided to wait patiently until tomorrow to ride Phil's new bicycle.

The next morning, Phil and Tommy went to the park and they took turns riding.

If Tommy had told his mother that Phil was being mean, then Phil might have had a very unhappy birthday.

If Tommy had draped toilet paper all over Phil's bike, Phil might have been very angry at Tommy!

Do you think Tommy made a good choice?
Why do you think that?

The Big Game

Marta is the goalie for her soccer team. It's an important game today, and the score is tied. Then, at the last minute, the other team scores a goal to win.

What do you think Marta should do?

Should Marta . . .

. . . congratulate the other team on a game well played?

. . . or throw her goalie gloves down angrily and storm off the field?

. . . or sit by herself and sulk while she eats all the snacks in the team's ice chest?

Which one would you choose?
Why would you choose that?

Marta decided to be a good sport and congratulated the other team on a great game.

Her teammates told her not to feel bad about missing the goal. They said she was a really great goalie, and they were so happy to have her on the team.

If Marta had stormed off the field, her teammates might have thought she was being a bad sport.

If Marta had eaten all the snacks, her teammates might have been upset with her!

Do you think Marta made a good choice?
Why do you think that?

Karate Class

Liam and Linda take karate lessons together. Today they tested for their next belt level. Linda passed the test, but Liam did not. Liam is feeling frustrated and upset.

What do you think Liam should do?

Should Liam . . .

. . . quit karate class
and never go back?

. . . or watch lots of karate
movies? It's more fun to watch
karate than learn it anyway.

. . . or ask Linda to help
him work on his karate
moves and then try taking
the test again?

Which one would you choose?
Why would you choose that?

Liam asked Linda to help him. He worked very hard to prepare for taking the test again.

Linda's help and Liam's hard work paid off. He passed the test!

If Liam had quit class, he might have felt even worse when Linda passed the next level test.

If Liam had only watched karate movies, he might have grown old without ever earning more than a yellow belt.

**Do you think Liam made a good choice?
Why do you think that?**

Cookies

Charlotte helped her neighbor bring in his groceries. To thank her, the neighbor gave her a small plate of cookies he'd made this morning. He suggested that maybe Charlotte would like to share them with her little brother.

What do you think Charlotte should do?

Should Charlotte . . .

. . . offer a cookie to her brother but tell him they were made with garlic and onions, so they do not taste very good?

. . . or hide in the closet and eat the whole plate of cookies herself?

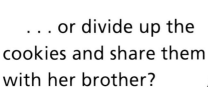

. . . or divide up the cookies and share them with her brother?

Which one would you choose?
Why would you choose that?

Charlotte remembered how good it feels when you share with others. She decided to share the cookies with her brother, just like her neighbor had suggested.

Charlotte and her brother each had one cookie and saved the rest of them to share later. They were delicious!

If Charlotte had convinced her brother that the cookies were made with garlic and onions, she might have felt bad for lying to her brother.

If Charlotte had eaten all the cookies by herself, she might have gotten sick!

Do you think Charlotte made a good choice?
Why do you think that?

Baby Sister

Noah's mom said she would play cards with him today, but his baby sister has come down with a bad cold. Mom says she's sorry, but things have changed, so she cannot play with Noah today after all.

What do you think Noah should do?

Should Noah . . .

. . . try to call up
his favorite superhero
to come and babysit,
saving the day?!

. . . or tell his mom it's
okay and make a date to
play cards another time,
when the baby feels better?

. . . or toss the cards
into the garbage can
and vow never to play
cards again?

Which one would you choose?
Why would you choose that?

Noah was unhappy about his plans changing, but he knew that his little sister needed his mom's attention. He told his mom it was okay and that they could play another time.

The next day his baby sister was feeling better, so Noah and his mom were able to play cards that afternoon.

If Noah had asked a superhero to help, the super-hero might not have known how to take care of a baby!

If Noah had thrown the cards into the garbage can, he might never have seen them again.

Do you think Noah made a good choice?
Why do you think that?

Playing Basketball

Sarah's three cousins are visiting today. Sarah really wants to play basketball, but the hoop is way too high for her youngest cousin.

What do you think Sarah should do?

Should Sarah . . .

. . . tell her young cousin to go and find something else to do?

. . . or try to put ten pairs of shoes on her young cousin to help her reach the hoop?

. . . or put away the basketball and find a game that everyone can play?

Which one would you choose?
Why would you choose that?

Sarah thought about what it feels like to be left out.

She chose to find a game they could all play, and everyone had fun!

If Sarah had told her young cousin to go away, her cousin might have been lonely and bored.

If she had tried to put ten pairs of shoes on her young cousin, her cousin might not have been able to stand up!

**Do you think Sarah made a good choice?
Why do you think that?**

Follow the Leader

Marcus and his friends are playing Follow the Leader.
Marcus loves being the leader, but now his turn is over.
It's Bret's turn to lead.

What do you think Marcus should do?

Should Marcus . . .

. . . play fair and let Bret take over as the leader?

. . . or find a way to keep Bret from stepping to the front of the line?

. . . or tell everyone what a bad leader Bret is so they won't want him to be the leader?

**Which one would you choose?
Why would you choose that?**

Marcus knows that playing fair is the right way to play.

He decided to step aside and let Bret take his turn as the leader.

If Marcus had refused to let Bret lead, the other kids might have been upset that he wasn't playing fair.

If Marcus had tried to convince everyone that Bret was a bad leader, he might have really hurt Bret's feelings.

Do you think Marcus made a good choice?
Why do you think that?

Field Trip

Jade's class is going on a field trip to the Natural History Museum tomorrow. Her teacher asks for everyone's attention so he can tell them some important information about the trip. Jade is drawing right now, and she doesn't want to stop to listen.

What do you think Jade should do?

Should Jade . . .

. . . keep drawing and hum loudly to block out her teacher's voice?

. . . or stop drawing and give the teacher her full attention?

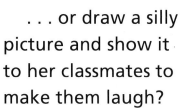

. . . or draw a silly picture and show it to her classmates to make them laugh?

Which one would you choose?
Why would you choose that?

Jade knew that what the teacher had to say was important. She decided to stop drawing and listen.

The next day, she had everything she needed for a great day at the museum.

If Jade had kept drawing and humming, she might not have heard that she was supposed to bring a sack lunch to the museum.

If Jade had made her classmates laugh, they might not have heard that they would see realistic, moving dinosaurs—and that could be scary if you didn't know they weren't real!

Do you think Jade made a good choice?
Why do you think that?

If you liked **What Would You Do?** here are some other
We Both Read® books you are sure to enjoy!

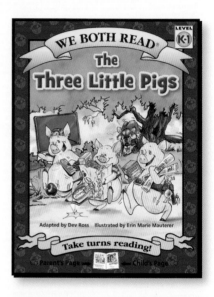

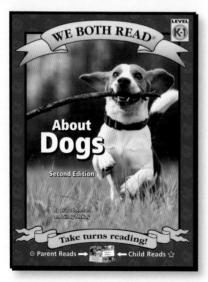

To see all the We Both Read books that are available,
just go online to **WeBothRead.com**.